What to Do While You Count to 10

Manage your Anger -

Change your Life

David W. Earle, LPC

First Edition – 2011

Second Edition - 2014

Copyright © 2011 by David W. Earle, LPC

Library of Congress Control Number: 2011901630

ISBN-13: 978-1491221440

ISBN-10: 1491221445

Table of Contents

Dedication

I would like to dedicate this book to all the people I have ever harmed with my unmanaged anger, especially my daughter, Ginger, and son, Garrett.

During the writing of this book, my granddaughter, Whitney Dean, who was adopted at birth, has reconnected with our family and a hole in my heart was healed with her arrival. I thank her wonderful parents who raised her and are now woven into the fabric of my life.

I could not have completed this project without the loving encouragement of Penny, my wife. Her laughter at my grammatical mistakes kept my head from expansion. She told me the first edition sounded like one of my lectures; that was valuable feedback so I rewrote it with a twinkle in my eye. Penny embraced this project and she is as much a part of this book as I am.

And Thanks

I owe my gratitude to the "Book Committee" for their valuable insight, humor, and most of all, encouragement.

The committee members are: David Abbott, Michael Atchison, Marc Biondo, Bob Breaux, Graeme Crawford, Dennis Daigle, Garrett Earle, Connie Fabre, Bill Golden, Summer Johnson, Judith Kenyon, Bob Leibforth, Vint Massimini, Connie & Ralph Murphy, Jonathan Repa, Janet Repa, Bill Schulenberg, Ron Schenk, Bob Slaven, Van Landry, Donna Freeman and Jan Zeringue.

Out of that group, I would like to make special mention. I received a very encouraging note from Jan Zeringue; arriving at a moment of extreme doubt. My two Florida friends' challenging comments really made me think, Bob Leibforth and Bob Slaven. My sister Connie and her husband Ralph Murphy gave me their feedback when I visited them in Virginia and I read their many suggestions at 30,000 feet returning to Louisiana. Bill Schulenberg was the grammar cop who faithfully prepared this book for the professional editor. Bill's spirit left this earth before he could see the result of his influence and I miss his wisdom and friendship.

I had two outside consultants: Trent Didier did the graphic design on the illustrations and book cover and Cliff Carle (the Sherlock Holmes of Editing) did the professional editing, both were instrumental in the ultimate outcome of this book.

Introduction

Counting to Ten Myth

When anger is used correctly, it can have positive results! However, this is a strange reality for some people. If you had told me during the first half of my life that there is a positive side to anger, I would have thought you were crazy.

All of us have witnessed anger destroying relationships, pushing people away, causing pain and hardship. Thinking about anger in positive terms is alien in most people's experiences. However, a healthy expression of anger is a component for building and maintaining successful relationships! If you want to use anger in a healthy and constructive manner, this book contains techniques necessary for that change. People who manage their emotions are calmer, the people they love are happier; and this book provides a blueprint for that change.

As a little boy, when I would get angry, my mother would say, "Count to ten". Try as I might, I could not make this advice work for me. By the time I reached the number ten, I was madder than when I started!

Numerous attempts at managing my anger by counting to ten continued well into my forties. With my long history of blowing my top, I often hurt the very people I loved the most. I knew I had to change.

Over 25 years of working as a therapist helping my clients manage their anger, I have discovered some powerful anger management tools. I will show you the coping skills necessary to change anger and other powerful and sometimes destructive emotions into a positive force for good. I had to learn what was necessary to do while I counted to ten and I now help others manage their emotions. The simple formula has proven successful for many of my clients.

When people use the lessons in this magical little book, they are able to express love instead of destruction. I firmly believe you are that person.

Is anger ever appropriate? Yes. What kind of anger is appropriate? Is anger selfish? Often it is considered selfish but what it really conveys is caring; if a person did not care, why would they be angry? Granted, anger can be misplaced and is often destructive, but anger generates passion, and that energy, if used correctly, can be highly constructive.

What about other emotions? Can this system work for the management of grief, revenge, jealousy, despair, etc.? Yes, this system is effective with the full rainbow of human emotions.

Setting the Conversation

On this adventure into anger management, you will experience mental health counseling sessions where two men discuss anger. The client has a very destructive anger problem and is devastated with the realization of the damage his anger has caused his family.

Although these characters assume different names to protect their anonymity, they are both real people and the dialogue is actual. Both have provided their permission to share this spotlight and they agreed to share this very personal experience with you.

Characters:

In these therapy sessions, Mr. Jack Walton is the mental health client and Mr. Eli Carlson is the licensed Professional Counselor.

Jack Walton is the client. Jack is a recently separated man in his early 40's with two children and a history of volatile anger that he acknowledges to be a significant part of the reason for the breakup of his marriage, and the estrangement from his children. Although no physical abuse occurred, he is aware of the emotional abuse his behavior caused.

His son went through treatment for substance abuse, but has recently relapsed back into his drug addiction. Jack is now attending the family portion of his son's treatment program, and is attending weekly Al-Anon meetings where he is learning how to deal with his son's substance abuse problem and how to develop healthy relationship skills. Jack recognizes he has a severe anger problem that needs to be changed. At this moment, he is unaware of his daughter's addiction to alcohol and drugs.

Jack is a successful executive, but the severe economic downturn has substantially affected his earnings. Because of his company's current financial trouble, he was terminated, ending a 10-year employment history.

His 20-year marriage was always rocky. Both he and his wife misused their anger and other strong emotions, and this constant tension turned the love they once had into bitterness and disdain. Although he wants to reconcile with his wife, he knows the hostile atmosphere they created is not good for the healthy exchange of love that he desperately craves, but doesn't know how to obtain.

Jack is a good man with a bad temper; a man who has a great deal of love in his heart, but his strong unmanaged emotions keep getting in the way, and cause his love to be destructive, exactly the opposite of want he wanted.

Both his teenage children are acting out with alcohol, drugs, truancy, and sexual activity. With the loss of his employment, he is experiencing intense financial pressure that has significantly contributed to the fracturing of his family. He feels guilty and blames himself for all that has happened to his family.

Eli Carlson, LPC is the counselor. Eli specializes in anger management, substance abuse treatment, and relationship issues, He is in his mid-60's, once divorced, and currently enjoying his second marriage of almost 20 years. Many years ago, he experienced a very intense anger problem that he has since learned to manage.

Setting:

They meet in an old house converted to an office building on a busy street located in the state capital of a Deep South state. They previously had a consultation visit where Jack's background information was obtained and a degree of trust was established. The story opens with Jack's first actual counseling session with Eli.

Chapter I

The Gift of Anger

First counseling session—September 30th

ELI: Good seeing you again.

JACK: I'm glad I'm back. I now realize that I am a large part of my problems, and more importantly, no one can change them but me. What is on the agenda today?

ELI: Whatever you want to work on.

JACK: Well, until I learn how to control my anger, I will continue to piss everyone off!

ELI: Well then, should we start on anger management today?

JACK: Anger management? Isn't that an oxymoron?

ELI: Although they may seem to be conflicting, they actually belong together. Let's talk about why anger is a human trait. Why were we created with the ability to get angry?

JACK: Beats me. Anger never worked for me. When I get angry, it seems to hurt everyone, and doesn't do any good.

ELI: Do you think the ability to get angry is something good, or something evil . . . even something demonic?

JACK: I know no good has come from my anger! I get depressed when I think about the harm it has done to my family.

I'm sure it contributed to the failure of my marriage, and I know I've harmed my kids.

ELI: You've certainly paid a high price for your anger.

JACK: Yes . . . you can say that again . . . for both me and the people I harmed.

ELI: What does anger do for us? Is there any value in anger, and if so, what is it?

JACK: "Do for us"? Come on, Eli, I'm paying good money for these sessions! Anger does something for us. Forgive my sarcasm, but does anger make our wives love us more? Do our children think we are "cuddly" and "cute" when we shout at them? Is that what you mean?

ELI: No, I was thinking something more in the positive sense. Can anger somehow build a relationship? You certainly seem to have experience with the opposite effect.

JACK: Yeah, I really blew it. It was my entire fault. That is why she left me. Sometimes I wish there was a way to remove my anger—permanently!

ELI: Can anger ever be positive?

JACK: I have never seen it.

ELI: Anger provides two benefits. There are two reasons why we need anger. Two reasons why humans have the ability to get angry.

JACK: Two? Benefits?

ELI: Yeah, two benefits. Could you survive in this world without the ability to get angry?

JACK: I think I'd like to try.

ELI: Okay, maybe it is not the anger itself, but how we use the anger that is the problem. Let's talk about what would happen if a person did not have the ability to get angry.

JACK: I'd like some of that!

ELI: Before you sign up for losing your ability to get angry, you might want to hear this:

Before the invention of psychotropic drugs, back in the 30's and 40's, in mental health hospitals, there was very little doctors could do for a violent patient—other than put them in straight jacks and confine them to padded cells.

Doctors believed they had no other choice than to perform what's called a frontal lobotomy. The operation consisted of cutting the nerves to the frontal lobes, the area of the brain that experiences feelings.

JACK: Maybe that's what I need . . . a frontal lobotomy. No feelings.

No anger. Simple, problem solved!

ELI: It's only used now in extreme cases, and your anger does not qualify, The key for you is the management of emotions, not the elimination.

Now, getting back to the old mental health wards—after the operation, the patients could not get angry. You could slap them in the face and they would register no emotion. That operation allowed them to be cared for in the mental health hospital, but could that person survive on the street?

JACK: I don't think so.

ELI: Of course not. Anger is a key survival tool in any culture with any group of people. So, anger does two things for us. First, anger is an early warning system. Anger is your radar for incoming insults, threats, or other attacks. Without this radar, we could not react in time, and might be consumed by today's equivalent of Tyrannosaurus Rex.

JACK: So you're saying I couldn't survive without anger.

ELI: Correct, you need your anger to protect yourself.

The key word is manage, Jack. You need the ability to get angry. But just because you are angry doesn't mean you have to continue to hurt the people you love.

JACK: I really don't believe you. Sorry.

ELI: Quite all right, just don't discount what I am saying. Try not to judge it.

JACK: Okay . . . just trust you . . . as in "The check is in the mail"?

ELI: Good one, but yes, you can trust me!

Once the anger alerts us to the threat on our radar screen, the second gift of anger is the necessary energy to deal with the attack. Should I fight or should I run? Do I need to face T. Rex head-on or run for my life? Just like the fight or flight syndrome, anger is natural. It is another way we respond to threats, or perceived slights, offenses, etc. What are some of the symptoms of anger?

JACK: You mean like yelling and screaming.

ELI: Yes, those are definite signs of anger. What I was thinking about were symptoms such as a rush of adrenalin, shortness of breath, racing heart, temperature change, muscle tension, clenched fists, agitation, and shaking.

JACK: Oh yeah, like when I'm angry I clench my teeth, it causes my jaw muscles to ache.

ELI: Exactly.

JACK: I grind my teeth at night. Is that a sign?

ELI: Anger is one of the causes. And when anger is triggered it evokes some or all of these other emotions: irritation, tension, frustration, hurt, fear and rage. Those strong emotions often are the reasons people can act aggressively, out of control, and say or do something that is not normal for them, which they later regret.

JACK: Do you have an example of how it can be used correctly? I am still having trouble seeing any merits to anger.

ELI: Do you remember seeing Dr. Martin Luther King and his followers marching in Selma, Alabama during the Civil Rights Movement back in the 60's? People my age watched it on small black and white TV sets where we had to adjust the rabbit ears to get the reception just right.

JACK: Is that when they came over that bridge and all the cops, with fire hoses and guard dogs, attacked them?

ELI: That is what I was remembering. Can you imagine the courage it must have taken, walking arm-in-arm off that bridge, singing "We Shall Overcome", and marching into that sea of angry white faces?

JACK: Yeah, that would have taken guts.

ELI: Yes, I don't know if I could have been that courageous marching off the Pettis Bridge. Their basic desire was for a better life with equality and respect. The energy that propelled these courageous people was their collective anger. Black people had hundreds of years of abuse, and it was that anger that gave them the necessary courage. This residual store of anger provided the energy they needed to demonstrate their plight to the world.

They were not armed, nor did they wish to inflict harm on those who tormented them. They used this anger to summon the courage and strength to stand up for themselves. In this case, anger was used correctly.

JACK: Okay, I never thought about that.

ELI: Mahatma Gandhi used that same collective nonviolent anger in the fight to gain independence from Great Britain after the Second World War.

So, back to my point: to have a successful relationship you need anger.

JACK: In that case, my marriage was a resounding success! I had a lot of anger!

ELI: The operative word in using anger to build relationships is correctly. What you experienced was allowing anger to destroy your love. The anger in itself was not the problem. The lack of anger management and the inappropriate expression of this anger is what doomed your relationship . . . sucked the love right out of it!

JACK: "Sucked the love out" is definitely correct. So . . . can you show me how to control my anger?

ELI: Let's discuss a time that you lost it because of your anger. Think of a time you got angry—a memorable time that you lost it

Exhibit I

T.I.E. - Anger Management Model

JACK: Okay, my teenage daughter was going to sneak out of the house one night, and her older brother tipped me off about her intentions. I waited downstairs and when she reached the door, I surprised her, and began yelling and screaming. I'll never forget the look on her face as she ran for her room . . . total fear. She shrunk into a corner with a look of absolute terror on her face.

As I look back on that experience, the sad part is the satisfaction I felt about how well I'd taught her this lesson. Time would prove that I had not, but at that moment, I was sure she would never try this again.

ELI: Jack, look at this feelings chart, and under the MAD column, tell me what emotions you were experiencing when you caught your daughter attempting to sneak out.

MAD	GLAD	SAD	FEAR	HURT
	Affection	Agonized	Anxious	Ashamed
Angry	Ardor	Bored	Apprehension	Belittled
Annoyed	Confident	Crushed	Bashful	Burdened
Antagonism	Cordiality	Deflated	Bewildered	Cheated
Arrogant	Curiosity	Depressed	Cautious	Contempt
Bitter	Delight	Disconnected	Confused	Denied
Contempt	Desire	Disparaged	Distraction	Deserted
Defiant	Devotion	Distant	Dread	Disappointed
Disapproving	Ecstasy	Distraught	Embarrassed	Dismay
Disdain	Ecstatic	Distressed	Envious	Embarrassed
Disgust	Elation	Downcast	Evasive	Exhausted
Disgusted	Enthusiasm	Forlorn	Fearful	Guilty
Enraged	Excitement	Gloomy	Flustered	Humiliated
Flustered	Fervor	Grieving	Frightened	Hurt
Frustrated	Flush	Helpless	Horrified	Insulted
Furious	Generosity	Hopeless	Hysterical	Lonely
Hostile	Happy	Ignored	Inadequate	Mean
indignant	Hope	Isolated	Insecure	Pain
Irritated	Hopeful	Jealous	Menaced	Pained
Livid	Inspiration	Melancholy	Overwhelmed	Regret
Mad	Love-Struck	Miserable	Panic	Shame
Mischievous	Passion	Mournful	Pathos	Suffering
Rage	Pride	Remorse	Shock	
Resentful	Sympathy	Sad	Shocked	
	Thrilled	Unwanted		

JACK: Angry. Disapproving. Enraged. Furious. Hostile, Rage . .
. yeah, lots and lots of rage!

ELI: Now, look at the chart and see what feelings you might
have had that are listed under the columns of H URT, SAD, and
FEAR.

JACK: Just angry . . . really angry!

ELI: Humor me, Jack. Put yourself back in that moment and look at the FEAR column. See anything that you might have been feeling?

JACK: Okay, I was alarmed. I mean, she was a teenage girl . . . it was the dead of night.

ELI: Alarm. Okay, what else? And in this discussion you don't have to explain your feelings, just identify them.

JACK: Alarmed. Fearful. Frightened. . . . Horrified. And in the HURT column: Burdened, Disappointed, and Pained. Is disrespected on this list?

ELI: No, it is not, however your experiencing disrespect is important. But let's put that aside for a few minutes. Alarmed. Fearful. Frightened. Horrified. Burdened, Disappointed, and Pained. I am going to use the T.IE. Anger Management Model and I'll explain what the "T.I.E." means later but here are the emotions you listed:

Exhibit II

T.I.E. – Anger Management Model

- Angry,
- Disapproving
- Enraged
- Furious
- Hostile
- Rage

- Burdened
- Disappointed
- Pained

ELI: You had the event, your daughter trying to sneak out, and then you had the feelings. Now, if we are not careful, we tend to have a reaction.

JACK: I had a reaction all right!

ELI: When we react emotionally, we often say or do something that we later regret, and probably would not have done if we were not so emotionally charged. Exhibit III shows the reaction.

T.I.E. – Anger Management Model

Exhibit III

- Angry,
- Disapproving
- Enraged
- Furious
- Hostile
- Rage

- Alarmed
- Fearful
- Frightened
- Horrified
- Burdened
- Disappointed
- Pained

JACK: I really hurt her with my reactions. . . my anger was an explosion! That is what made me realize that something was wrong with me . . . like I was some kind of a monster.

ELI: Emotional reactions can be very destructive. When we allow our emotions to control us, then we react as in "E over I" . . . Emotions over Intellect.

T.I.E. – Anger Management Model

Exhibit IV

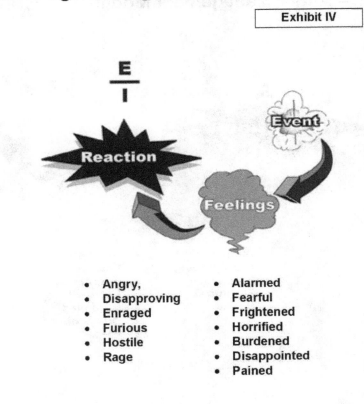

- Angry,
- Disapproving
- Enraged
- Furious
- Hostile
- Rage

- Alarmed
- Fearful
- Frightened
- Horrified
- Burdened
- Disappointed
- Pained

JACK: So the "E" in this model stands for our emotions and the "I" stands for intellect—how we think?

ELI: Yes. When a person's emotions are in control, it is very similar to a person who is inebriated. For the purposes of this lesson, people who are "E over I" we are going to call "emotionally drunk". Even when a person has not had alcohol in 20 years, they still can be "emotionally" drunk when their emotions are in control.

JACK: I see. I was hurting the people I loved with my emotions so badly, they had to join me! We all were emotionally drunk.

ELI: Your love was real, but because you were not managing your emotions, the love you were trying to express came out as "Nazi nurturing."

JACK: Yes, I see. I wanted to express the nurturing love of a father, but the way it came out is not the way I wanted . . . like a Nazi Storm Trooper.

ELI: Sometimes when we are trying to do our best, we end up doing the wrong thing—often for the right reasons.

JACK: My heart says what I was trying to do was right, but my mind can't let go of the image—that look on her face. I wish I could take it all back. But I can't. Just talking about it is helping, though.

ELI: Good. Getting honest about what is in our heads and in our hearts provides some relief to the pain and shame we experienced in these situations.

JACK: Spilling my guts helps?

ELI: Yes, honesty is very cathartic. One of the slogans of a 12-Step program is "We are as sick as our secrets." Okay, if being "E over I" is where we don't want to be, let's now discuss where we want to be.

I' m going to draw a big "X" over the E over I. (See Exhibit V)

T.I.E. – Anger Management Model

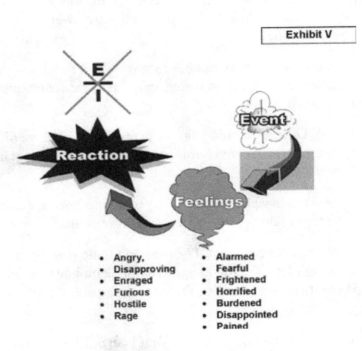

Exhibit V

- Angry,
- Disapproving
- Enraged
- Furious
- Hostile
- Rage

- Alarmed
- Fearful
- Frightened
- Horrified
- Burdened
- Disappointed
- Pained

ELI: Okay, tell me, what happens in your brain between the actual event and the feelings?

JACK: I'm not sure if I understand you. ELI: I'll put it another way: your feelings . . . your emotions, what are they based upon? What is happening in your head that is causing these feelings?

JACK: Expectations?

ELI: Close. How about thoughts? Your feelings and emotions are based upon your thoughts. Two people can witness the same event and have two different thoughts about it, which can create different emotions.

T.I.E. - Anger Management Model   Exhibit VI

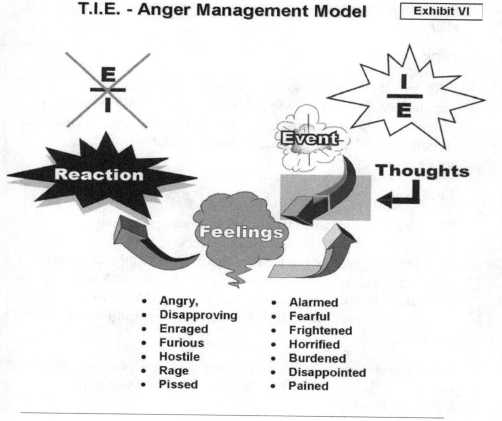

- Angry,
- Disapproving
- Enraged
- Furious
- Hostile
- Rage
- Pissed

- Alarmed
- Fearful
- Frightened
- Horrified
- Burdened
- Disappointed
- Pained

JACK: So, when I have feelings, they are based upon thoughts.

ELI: Correct. Now, think back to the third grade when you studied icebergs. You found out that ninety percent of the iceberg is under the water. The expression "tip of the iceberg" refers to that part of the iceberg that's out of the water, what we can see. Emotions are like the iceberg with anger being the tip. When a person is angry, it is often the anger that is so visible and easily observed. However, beneath the anger there are other feelings driving the anger.

Take your example: in the experience you had with your daughter sneaking out, you were, by your own account very angry.

JACK: I'll say.

ELI: I wrote down the words you used to describe what you were feeling. They all were found in the MAD column. You listed, "Angry, Disapproving, Enraged, Furious, Hostile, Rage". These emotions are what your daughter observed that night. She saw your anger.

JACK: Yes.

ELI: For the purpose of this exercise, the angry feelings you expressed are the tip of the emotional iceberg. Let's ignore these emotions, and explore the feelings that were driving that strong anger reaction. What emotions are under the anger? A little while ago, I wrote down that you said you were "Alarmed, Fearful, Frightened, Horrified, Burdened, Disappointed, and Pained".

Now, take off the anger words in your list and pick out one or two of the other emotions that best describe what you were feeling that night.

JACK: Afterwards, when I reflected upon that night, it was the Pain and Shame. However, when I caught her sneaking out, well it was Fear. That is the best word to describe it—just a lot of Fear.

ELI: You felt the shame after the event, but during the sneaking out caper you felt fear. Now, in order to get to the thought, you need a certain realization and it comes in a two-part sentence.

The first part of the sentence is: our feelings do not lie to us. Whatever you are feeling . . . you are feeling! Now, I will get to the second part in a few minutes.

Some people may attempt to squash your feelings with statements such as "You're not really feeling that way!" or "You shouldn't feel that way"! The truth is, whatever you are feeling is yours and no one has the right to tell you how to feel.

JACK: I like that.

ELI: Is it okay for people to be angry?

JACK: Well, no . . . look at all the damage I caused.

ELI: Was it the anger that caused the problem, or was it how you expressed that anger?

JACK: How I expressed it.

ELI: All right then, is it okay to hurt someone when you are angry?

JACK: No.

Anger is a choice.

ELI: So, it's obvious that no one has the right to hurt someone else with their anger. Some people, however, are surprised to know that it is okay for us to be angry.

JACK: That's a shock to me!

ELI: Remember, you were born with the ability to get angry. Humans could not survive without it. You need your anger. Civilization just needs a better method for expressing this anger because hurting another person just because we have angry feelings cannot be justified. As simple as these concepts appear to be, many people have never thought it through and are confused with devastating results!

You keenly felt the destructive force of your anger, how it enslaved you with destructive results. Tell me, Jack, would you like some freedom?

JACK: Freedom? Yes.

ELI: Have you ever heard someone say, "He makes me so angry? "or "She really makes me mad?"

JACK: I say that all the time, people really can get my goat. I know people who consistently make me angry . . . like about half the drivers on the freeway.

ELI: Let me give you some wonderful information . . . some great freedom will come from knowing this.

JACK: I'm waiting.

ELI: Here it is: No one can "make" you angry! No one can "make" you mad!

JACK: Sorry, but I know some people who certainly can! My family knows my buttons and boy, can they push them!

ELI: Let me clarify what I just said. No one can make you angry without your permission. Don't get me wrong, some people give us great opportunity to be angry, especially our loved ones who know where all our buttons are located, and what reaction comes with each button they push. What I mean is that anger . . . your anger . . . is a *choice*! You can *choose* to be angry or you can *choose* not to be angry.

I remember when I first learned this profound wisdom. I did not believe it when I first heard it. I had spent forty-two years easily being angered.

So the idea that I had some degree of control over my anger was completely alien to my experiences. Even though I did not believe it, I was fortunate in that I did not discount that concept, for as life would have it, very shortly afterwards I had the chance to prove that concept for myself.

I locked my keys in the car! I felt that old rage come up inside me and I was ready to smash my car window. Looking back on my reaction, it's obvious that breaking the window didn't make sense. But at the time it was exactly what I wanted to do.

Then I somehow remembered to ask myself, "Do you really want to be angry about this, or not?" And I said, "No!" And I stopped being angry! I was then free. I knew then, that I could choose to be angry, or I could choose not to be angry. What freedom!

JACK: Wow! I never knew that I had a choice. If I can do that, if I can choose, you're right . . . that is freedom.

ELI: Okay, our time is up for today shall we make another appointment?

JACK: Can't wait.

Chapter 2

The Guiding Force of Emotions

Second counseling session—October 7th

JACK: Okay, Eli I'm back . . . ready to get my head shrunk!

ELI: Glad to have you back . . . and contrary to popular beliefs, I do not shrink heads.

JACK: I know you don't . . . just had to get my jab in early. What are we going to learn today?

ELI: Here is another simple yet profound idea. If someone else is angry, do you have to be angry?

I spent 20 years in a marriage where every time she got angry, I did too. As obvious as it seems on this side of discovery, I did not know that I had a choice to get angry or not when she did.

JACK: Me too! When she got angry, I did too.

ELI: Now for the second part of that sentence I wanted d to give you.

Your feelings do not lie to you was the first part.

To help us with the second part, try to remember a situation like this. Most people don't remember an exact instance of this, but all say they have had this experience. Have you ever had a friend that you got into an argument with, had hard feelings toward them, stomped away, and then did not speak to that person for a few days?

JACK: Of course.

ELI: Did you later discover that what you got mad about really didn't happen as you first thought?

JACK: Yeah.

ELI: Okay, when you got angry with your friend, your feelings of hurt and anger did not lie to you. However, those feelings were based upon a false thought.

Okay, the complete sentence I want you to have is: "Your feelings do not lie to you . . . however, they may be based upon one of three premises: (1) a false thought, something that is not true (2) something that is true, or (3) sometimes more information is needed."

In order to put the first and second part of the sentences together, you must understand that it is the thoughts that are driving the emotion . . . as shown in Exhibit VI. When using this sentence with our model, we can now judge our thoughts. Are they true? Are they false? Or do I need more information?

JACK: That answers my question about your feelings not lying to you.

Your feelings are true but the problem comes from thoughts that are not true. Using my example, if I feel confident, but if the thought providing that confidence is incorrect then that confidence is false and unrealistic.

ELI: Great. Once we understand what emotion(s) we are feeling, then they become our guides to recognize what thought(s) caused us those feelings.

JACK: I follow you.

Your feelings do not lie to you;
however, they may be based upon a false thought,
or a true thought,
or based upon incomplete information.

ELI: When using this technique, the emotions are the guide to discovering the thought driving the emotion. This allows decisions based upon logic and intellect instead of raw emotion. Just wallowing in feelings is being emotionally drunk. However, if we acknowledge and identify the emotions, they can return us to the thoughts that are creating the emotions.

A person's internal radar set is working when their emotions guide them back to the thoughts creating the emotions. Thoughts are the home of logic where better decisions are made.

JACK: So I can use my radar set to guide me?

ELI: Exactly. Now let's go back to that episode of your daughter sneaking out. What thoughts were driving that intense feeling of fear you had? Why were you afraid?

JACK: Well, she's a young kid, a girl, sneaking out in the middle of the night, to what I haven't a clue, but I can imagine. I'm guessing there was some boy involved.

I was trying to protect her. I thought if I could scare her, then maybe she wouldn't want to sneak out like that.

ELI: When I first asked you about your feelings concerning that night, if you remember, you said "disrespect"?

JACK: And you said to ignore it for a while.

ELI: Now it is time to add it to your list of thoughts. Did you think your daughter sneaking out was disrespectful of you?

JACK: Yes, most definitely.

ELI: So, while your thoughts were about her getting hurt and wanting to protect her, you also thought she was disrespecting you.

JACK: Yeah, that's it.

ELI: Challenge those thoughts: were they true thoughts, false thoughts, or did you need more information?

JACK: They are all true.

ELI: Once the emotions have guided you to your thought, you can challenge and judge your thoughts. When this is occurring, you have arrived at "I over E", Intellect over Emotions. Your rational mind is now managing your emotions. You are not emotionally drunk and reacting. You can now know what thoughts were driving your feelings.

JACK: So . . . our emotions can guide us to the thoughts that are the driving force of our behavior.

ELI: Well said.

JACK: Looking at the T.I.E. Model, I think I could have reacted differently if my rational mind were in control. (See Exhibit VI)

ELI: Most people have the same realization.

When you are in your rational mind, you are able to challenge your thinking. You can ask, "Is this thought true? Is it false? Do I need more information?"

"Is the thought that my daughter could face unknown dangers sneaking out at night a true thought, a false thought, or do I need more information?"

T.I.E. - Anger Management Model

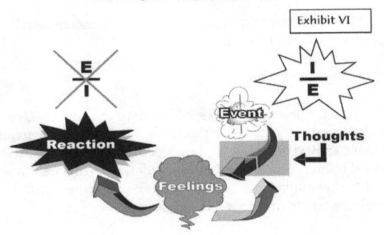

JACK: I think my thoughts on that night were absolutely true!

ELI: Now you can decide what to do about it. In your rational mind, you have the ability to make calm and well thought-out choices. When emotionally drunk you often act on impulse and the results are, at best, suspect.

JACK: "Suspect?" You have a gentle way of saying I screwed up . . . completely overreacted!

ELI: Are you sometimes too hard on yourself?

JACK: Most of the time. And usually I deserve it!

ELI: Are you now "emotionally drunk" about yourself?

JACK: Own! That hurts . . . but it's true.

ELI: In our rational minds, we can now challenge our thoughts. Just then, what feeling did you have about yourself?

JACK: Anger, bitterness, disgust, contempt, hate, you want more?

ELI: What thoughts are driving that hate? What is the hate based upon?

JACK: I'm a no good SOB! I screwed up my marriage, screwed up my kids, I'm worthless . . .I can't do anything right!

ELI: Let's challenge that. What part of screwing up your marriage is true?

JACK: She left me, didn't she? I must be worthless, discarded trash! That's what she thinks, that's what I think.

ELI: In the light of day, were all the problems of your marriage your fault? Were you, alone, responsible for the negativity your children received?

JACK: Of course it wasn't my entire fault, but I'm the man in the family, and I should have handled it differently.

ELI: Therefore, what is bothering you is the way you handled it.

JACK: Yeah, my behavior.

ELI: If you had to do it over again, would you have done it the same way?

JACK: No, of course not.

ELI: Now that you are in your rational mind and you can make a better determination, ask yourself: "What part of this problem is mine and what do I need to work on? What part is someone else's problem, and what part are they responsible for changing?"

When you do that, it allows you to have the freedom . . . the freedom to change.

JACK: I think I get it. Get out of being emotionally drunk . . . towards myself . . . and instead get into my rational mind. When I am emotionally sober, I can make decisions based upon facts and not emotional reactions.

ELI: "Boom goes the dynamite!"

JACK: Funny! Where did that come from?

ELI: Will Smith, the actor, say it when he made a mistake; I think it sounds kind of cool.

JACK: "Boom goes the dynamite" . . . sounds like my anger explosion!

ELI: The three parts of this model are as follows; Feeling, Thoughts, and Action.

What am I feeling? What thoughts are driving those feelings? What am I going to do about it?

Let me tell you a couple of stories about "I over E". A young man who came to see me had stolen a jet ski, and his parents thought it would be a good idea if he had some counseling before appearing before the judge. One of the topics we worked on was this exact model. The judge sentenced him to thirty days in the juvenile justice system. After his release, he came back to see me and told me this story.

He said that for most of his life, his coping skills could best be described as "E over I"—emotionally drunk. He knew, in the juvenile facility his poor coping skills would cause him more problems that he did not want.

Instead of his normal emotionally drunk behavior, when confronted by potentially destructive emotions and reacting in an emotionally drunk manner; he repeated this phrase to himself again and again: "I over E" . . . "I over E" . . . "I over E". That mantra was successful for that young man, and I'm sure he wouldn't mind if you used it as your reminder not to become emotionally drunk.

JACK: If I just say it over and over, will it really work?

ELI: It has worked for many others. Here is the other story; a couple came to me because of anger issues with their son. In their first visit, I found out that Mom had an anger problem as well as Dad. Junior learned it from two experts! I made an appointment with Dad on a Thursday and scheduled Junior on Friday afternoon. In Dad's session, we worked on the "I over E" model.

The next morning I got a phone call from Dad. That night, Junior had pitched one of his famous temper tantrums, physically attacked his mother, and was arrested for his behavior. As Dad described how out of control his son was, and that his wife was right in the middle, he told me that he was amazingly calm . What kept him calm was repeating the mantra to himself, "I over E". That simple saying worked wonders for him!

Later that afternoon when I visited with Junior, I showed him this same model, and then asked, "Do you think, "I over E", will work for you? In his seventeen-year-old wisdom, he said, "No!"

I said, "Last night was rough for you."

He responded with, "Yeah, I didn't mean to hurt my mother, but she made me so mad!" As he described this incident, his pent up emotions kicked in and he got angry all over again.

When I asked what his mother was doing, he said, "She was in my face, yelling, and I was hollering back".

When I asked him what Dad was doing, a strange look came over his face. Junior replied, "He was calm!"

"Oh, so he was calm?" I reiterated "And is he usually like?" Junior was again animated and said, "Oh, he'd be in my face, yelling, pushing me . . . just daring me to hit him."

I asked, "Do you know what he was thinking then?"

He said, "No, what?"

I said, "He was thinking . . .'I over E'"!

A smile of recognition came over his face and let loose with a big smile. He finally got it.

So Jack, this simple little formula works when it is used. You always have the ability to be "emotionally drunk". However, when you can add "I over E" to your emotional toolbox, now you have another choice.

JACK: Wow, so it really does work!

ELI: It worked for that family. Nine months later, I had the occasion to ask Dad if he was still emotionally sober. He grinned and said, "Yes, sober . . . although I had a few buzzes!"

JACK: Emotional buzz, I live with a perpetual emotional buzz!

ELI: I hope you now know you have a choice. Do you want to live with an emotional buzz or be emotionally sober? It's your choice.

JACK: I've been emotionally drunk for over forty years, I think I'll try being emotionally sober for the next forty. When I'm eighty then I can decide which worked better for me!

ELI: One last story: A client who works for a building supply store said that on a frustrating day, with many more customers than salespeople, he was at the register besieged with a myriad of different demands. He was quietly saying aloud to himself "I over E" . . . "I over E" in his attempt to stay emotionally sober.

A puzzled customer looked at him and asked, "Instrumentation over Electrical?" My client laughed to himself, and then said, "Yeah, I'm hoping we have a big sale in those departments".

JACK: Many people seem to be getting benefits from "I over E." I sure hope I do.

ELI: You will.

JACK: So in reality this technique is not just for anger management. It can be used for all feelings?

ELI: Absolutely. Recently, a client told me of her irritation toward her aging mother when her mom repeated herself. We put this experience through this same model and discovered that under the feeling of irritation, this woman was feeling fear. Once she understood it was fear driving her irritation, she then discovered the thought causing the fear. She realized it was when her mother showed her age, she knew someday soon she was going to lose her mother, her mother was going to die. That thought scared her. Her irritation was really a misdirected expression of love that came out as irritation and impatience toward her mother.

JACK: I guess that is like the Nazi nurturing you talked about, having loved come out in hurtful ways.

I can see my time is up for today. But before I go, I'm going to give myself a homework assignment and try this "I over E" tool. See you next week.

ELI: I look forward to hearing how it turns out.

We are as sick as our secrets.
12- Step slogan

Chapter 3

Fingers vs. Thumbs

Third counseling session — October 15th

JACK: Good morning, what's in store for today?

ELI: How did your homework work out? Did you use the "I over E" since our last session?

JACK: I thought about it . . . but only after I lost it.

ELI: Tell me what happened.

JACK: I got so angry with my son. He stole about three hundred dollars from me.

ELI: So you got angry.

JACK: Yeah, don't I have the right to get angry when someone steals from me?

ELI: Just because we are learning to manage our emotions doesn't take away our right to have emotions.

JACK: Well, I had all of them and then invented a few emotions of my own. I was so shocked and disappointed. When I found out what he had done, I changed the locks on the apartment.

ELI: You made a statement to him that his behavior was not acceptable.

JACK: Is that what I did? I wanted to hit him.

ELI: But you didn't.

JACK: No.

ELI: What made you think you "lost it"?

JACK: I was hollering and screaming, ranting and raving like a mad man. Then I remembered "I over E".

ELI: And what happened then?

JACK: That's when I calmed down and had the locks changed.

ELI: So you didn't use this model perfectly, you didn't remember until after you "lost it".

JACK: Yeah.

ELI: Jack, I think you had a successful learning experience. Often it's when we fall down that we begin to learn. Isn't that how you learned to ride a bike . . . by falling down?

JACK: Well, I guess you're right because after that incident, every time I started to lose it, your voice popped into my mind and I could hear you saying, "I over E". . . "I over E". . . "I over E". And it was just as you said with that little saying, I could now choose whether I wanted to lose it or not! Amazing!

ELI: Good, I am glad it worked for you.

JACK: I also realized that this technique is good for managing any emotion, not just anger.

ELI: You got it.

JACK: Where did this T.I.E. Anger Management System come from?

ELI: I believe the basic format came from a Divorce Adjustment Seminar I attended in Houston, Texas. Where they got it I don't know. I've modified and added to it over the years.

JACK: Where does T.I.E. mean?

ELI: Oh, my friend Bill Schulenberg thought up that name. It stands for: "Think I over E as in T.I.E.

JACK: I feel much more empowered. Now I can make this anger thing work for me instead of against me.

ELI: You are much more powerful when managing your emotions. Today, we are going to work on: Half the battle of life.

JACK: Excuse me?

ELI: This one sentence I'm about to give you, contains a technique that helps people achieve a successful life, all this in one short sentence.

JACK: That's a promise I'd like to see you fulfill.

ELI: There is a little catch, however.

JACK: I thought as much.

ELI: The catch is . . . you'll have to change. You'll have to incorporate this little sentence, or mantra, into your thinking, and live the message as part of your coping skills, if you want the full benefit.

JACK: Okay, I'm game.

ELI: Here's the sentence . . . drum roll please . . .
JACK: Rat-ta-tat, rat-ta-tat, rat-ta-tat, rat-ta-tat.

ELI: "My Life Will Change When I Change."™ Although I was not the first person to make that statement, I thought it summed up my life's motto so well that I had it trademarked.

JACK: Really?

ELI: Not that I wanted exclusive rights to that coping skill, I just wanted to market the life changes I advocated under a unifying statement.

JACK: It is a powerful statement.

ELI: That little sentence is at least one-half of the battle of life. And as in most simple concepts, there is a great deal of hidden depth within the application. In the mental health field, the definition of this concept is known as "Locus of Control".

ELI: A person with an external "Locus of Control" thinks their success and their happiness is somewhere outside of themselves. All romantic notions are predicated on some prince in shining armor, or a fair damsel, will bring us the happiness we seek. As wonderful as this person may be, no other human being can bring us happiness.

When we find a wonderful person who makes us happy, we marry them, and live happily ever after, right?

JACK: Yeah, right!

ELI: And this happiness happens just like our culture promises . . . for a while anyway . . . then reality sets in!

JACK: Yeah, I know about reality. My roommate, John Williams, is a songwriter and one of his lyrics is, "When reality hits, it's not always what we want it to be." I know I did not make my wife happy, yet I think that she married me because she thought I would make her happy.

ELI: That is not uncommon. In fact, I would say it is true in most cases. Were you ever able to make your wife happy?

JACK: I did for the first three days of our marriage, and then reality set in. I failed and she got angry, and then stayed angry for twenty years.

ELI: That is a long time. At the beginning of our discussion, didn't you take all the blame for the breakup of the marriage?

JACK: Yeah, I did. Just as she thought, I should make her happy.

Now that I think about it, I assumed that was my job . . . to make her happy. I got irritated when I disappointed her, and then she got angry, so I got angry. Kind of screwed up, weren't we?

ELI: Until we step back and look at the system we're in, it's very hard to see what is happening. Screwed up? I'd say your pattern is unfortunately all too normal. We humans are locked into these patterns of expectations and disappointments. And whom do we attack if they don't come true?

JACK: The people we love the most . . . I know that answer!

ELI: When the happily-ever-after fairy tale explodes, Prince Charming and the Fair Damsel come to me for marriage counseling . . . often too late. Boiled down, their basic complaint is that "He is not making me happy." Or, "She is not living up to my expectations of the magical bliss her feminine wiles so promised." They point at one another and declare, "Not fair. This person I married is not making me happy!"

They don't use those particular words, but underneath many matrimonial discords are these exact thoughts.

JACK: You've hit the nail on the head.

ELI: I am labeling this behavior "finger pointing". It happens when we look outside of ourselves, pointing the finger and shifting the blame. Their finger pointing is a perfect example of an "External Locus of Control". With this mindset, their happiness is invested outside of themselves in someone else.

JACK: We did a lot of finger pointing!

ELI: Easy to do. Another way of saying that is "taking someone else's inventory".

JACK: Like saying, "You know what your problem is . . . !"

ELI: Good example. We bring our empty bucket of unmet needs to another and expect them to fill it. As wonderful as this person may be, they are inadequate to fill our empty bucket. They can dash some water in it, or sprinkle in a few raindrops, but they are incapable of filling that bucket.

We had these expectations of how wonderful life was going to be and that failed to be realized.

JACK: I tend to get down on myself when I fail.

ELI: Do you see yourself as making a mistake, or do you see it as being a mistake?

JACK: Oh, I see that I am a mistake, but maybe that is really not correct, is it?

ELI: There is a big difference between the two, as divergent as the difference in being sad and happy.

JACK: That makes sense. I expected to make her happy, she expected me to make her happy, and when I did not, I saw myself as a failure, and she certainly saw me as a failure.

ELI: One of the wonderful sayings found in 12- Step programs is "Expectations are resentments under construction!"

JACK: That's a good one.

ELI: And how do we express our dissatisfaction ... this pervasive feeling of unrequited needs?

JACK: With anger of course!

ELI: That is a normal reaction and we often express this as destructive rage.

The opposite of finger pointing is looking at us! Turning it around and pointing our thumbs at ourselves. This is an "Internal Locus of Control" as in, "My Life Will Change ... When I Change." ™ This paradigm shift from external to internal, from finger pointing to thumb declaration is the hardest work we have to do. However, like most hard work, it is incredibly rewarding. I call this "Thumb Work".

JACK: So, Finger Work creates resentment and Thumb Work makes changes, right?

ELI: Well said. Now think of a person you have conflict with. Get someone firmly in mind. For most of us, that is easy to do.

JACK: Yeah, I'll focus on my ex-wife. She certainly fits the description of "difficult".

ELI: So, we'll label her a "difficult person". Now, what would happen if you changed this label?

JACK: Changed it to what?

ELI: Changed your description of this "difficult person" to . . . "your teacher"?

JACK: Seeing the Wicked Witch of the West as my teacher?

ELI: Yes, what would happen if you were to make this change and start seeing this so-called difficult person as someone who has something to teach you? Would there be a shift in your attitude?

JACK: My "ex" as my teacher? Yeah, if I made that change, I would see our relationship differently.

ELI: Would you have come in to see me if your relationship with her had not turned out like it did?

JACK: No, certainly not, I would not have come to counseling otherwise.

I guess you could say I was desperate when I walked through your door.

ELI: If she had not been the person she was, and if the breakup did not hurt so much, would you be here today?

JACK: No, it took the breakup to open my eyes.

ELI: Very good, Jack . . . Well, it's all the time we have for today . . . See you next week.

Focus on Thumbs,
not Fingers

Chapter 4

Radar Set

Fourth counseling session—October 21st

ELI: Comfortable, Jack? Okay . . . at birth, everyone gets a radar set called "feelings". Most people have never been taught to use this internal radar set. Many of us are unaware that we even have one!

Did you see the movie, Titanic? JACK: Who didn't?

ELI: The Titanic did not have radar, and ran into the iceberg with disastrous results. Not knowing how to use our radar . . . our feelings, causes us to run into life's icebergs. When we do not know how to use our emotions, we, like the Titanic, sink into the Sea of Despair.

The feeling language has five main words: Mad, Sad, Glad, Hurt, and Fear.

JACK: You remember, at our first session, when you first asked what I was feeling? I had a hard time identifying what I was experiencing. I think I was numb then. However, last night when I was returning from my AL-Anon meeting, I was crying big alligator tears.

There is so much pain in my life now. I do not often cry, but the strange part is that at the same time, I experienced a sense of joy or gladness. Isn't that weird? How can you have two completely different feelings at the same time?

ELI: You were feeling hurt and joy at the same time?

JACK: Yeah.

ELI: Were you emotionally numb at that time?

JACK: No, I had all strong feelings coming out all over.

ELI: Did you feel alive when you were numb?

JACK: Ah, now that I think about it, no. When I went numb it was like a color TV that suddenly changed to black and white.

ELI: So you were feeling pain last night?

JACK: Yeah. When I was numb, the pain wasn't so acute, but last night it was very painful. I felt the pain. I wasn't hiding anymore. Is that what it was? I was actually feeling my feelings. I felt alive! That was so much different from being numb. I felt the joy of now being alive . . . it was such a relief.

ELI: Wow! You allowed yourself to feel the pain, to become real, and you felt alive.

JACK: Yeah, numb no more!

ELI: It all started with those five words of the feeling language.
JACK: Mad, Glad, Sad, Fear, and Hurt.

ELI: You're learning well! The path of internal discovery is to claim our self-love, Self-worth begins with the Locus of Control pointed inward, thumb work. The portal to this inward journey is through the doorway of emotions.

JACK: Being emotionally numb kept me moving in the wrong direction, not real, not alive, and especially for me, incredibly unhappy.

ELI: You got it.

All decisions involve a large component of emotions often either overlooked or not dealt with. Just witness the stock market gyrations. Its excessive highs and lows are guided by either unbridled euphoria or the "sky is falling" fear mentality, neither proving true over time. These reactions are led by the feelings of euphoria or fear.

JACK: I lost a bunch of money in the stock market when Chicken Little cried, "The sky is falling", and I believed that damned chicken.

ELI: You had a lot of company.

I helped Gulf Coast petrochemical company's employees in their Louisiana refinery to improve their plant culture by changing from the command/control style to one that increased employee empowerment, responsibility, and communications. In a meeting with their senior directors, I asked them what they were feeling about the concept of empowering their employees.

JACK: You asked managers to express their feelings? I can't picture that. What response did you get?

ELI: Many expressed thoughts as opposed to feelings, as to why this will never work. But one got honest with the answer, "Stark raving fear!" Once that honest emotion was expressed, it gave everyone else permission to be emotionally honest. Then these managers began to deal with their fears.

JACK: I'd like to have been a fly on that wall!

ELI: Since all decisions involve a large component of emotions, often the very feelings that are driving these decisions lack acknowledgment, lack expression. The results are reactions to these hidden feelings rather than the cool calculated thought process. When emotions are not dealt with they are exhibited in unintentional and destructive behavior.

Knowing we have this hidden radar set capable of navigating through life is a powerful realization. When we begin to acknowledge our emotions, our radar set, and understand how it operates, we then have a powerful guidance system.

JACK: I guess I'll have to dig out the manual to my radar set!

ELI: Very good, Jack. Well, our time is up. See you next week.

Acknowledge feelings;
use your radar set.

Chapter 5

Command Phrases

Fourth counseling session—October 22nd

ELI: Okay, Jack, let's go back to the anger model again, and talk about command phrases. . . what we tell ourselves about a situation.

JACK: Sounds like self-talk, which I do a lot. Usually what I tell myself is negative.

ELI: Well, this time we have the power of decisions based upon knowledge, not *knee—jerk* reactions.

There are several categories of command language: withdrawal, outward, divert, internalize, and healthy.

Withdrawal is hiding from the threat, running away, or the inability to address the problem directly.

Withdrawal command phrases are expressed like this:
- "I can't deal with this"
- "This is dangerous"
- "I'm being attacked"
- "Let me out of here"

JACK: Like saying, "I'm out of here", or threatening to leave someone?

ELI: Exactly. Making threats you have no intention of carrying out, using them as a method to control others . . . for example, when couples use the threat of divorce to win the argument.

JACK: You nailed me . . . guilty on that count.

ELI: The outward focus is directing the energy toward another person and becoming the aggressor.

Outward command phrases may sound like this:
- "I'll show him"
- "You can't push me around"
- "It's not fair"
- "That #%@*$ jerk"
- "I hate him"
- I'll show her"

Another command phrase tactic is changing the subject, or ignoring the attack. This is attempting to divert, diffuse, or keep the energy from focusing.

Diverting command phrases often sound like this:
- "Can't you take a joke?"
- "I was only kidding"
- "My stomach hurts"

JACK: Oh, that is what she and I would do! We would make jokes about one another that were hurtful, and when the other would complain, we'd say "I was only kidding", or "What's the matter with you, don't you have a sense of humor?" Actually, they were verbal barbs. Were those expressions of anger?

ELI: What do you think?

JACK: I think they were. We weren't expressing our anger toward one another directly. Instead, we used this hurtful humor to express ourselves, throwing anger spears at one another.

ELI: Okay, the next category of command phrases is getting angry with you, resulting in self-abuse expressed as inner anger.

Self-abuse command phrases often take this form:
- "I'm wrong"
- "I'm no good"
- "I can't do anything right"
- "No one cares"
- "I always screw up"
- "No one could love me"

JACK: Playing the victim, I've done that.

ELI: Did it work?

JACK: I was a great victim, until now I could not understand why she said she lost respect for me. When she said that, it hurt more than when she told me we were through.

ELI: So what you're telling me, when you acted like a victim, she lost respect for you.

JACK: She never put it in those terms, and at that time I didn't see it that way, but yeah, that makes sense.

ELI: Your being a victim drove your wife away?

JACK: Yeah, that and my anger. Sad isn't it?

ELI: Very sad.

Now, contrast the first four categories of command language: withdrawal, outward, divert, and internalize with this last one, the healthy.

JACK: Healthy . . . that has a nice ring to it.

ELI: Yes, it's something we all are striving for. In the midst of your worst day when you screamed at your daughter, you were really trying to do the right thing.

JACK: I don't quite believe you, but man, do I want to! Wait a minute, if I accept that I really was trying to do the right thing, and then I would begin forgiving myself. Wow!

ELI: Good insight. Don't reject that notion of self-forgiveness; allow it to bubble through your consciousness.

JACK: Pardon?

ELI: It's an expression, but yeah, let it bubble through your thought process.

JACK: I'm bubbling!

ELI: Okay, since we are now talking about healthy, when a person's intellect is managing their emotions, as in "I over E", the reaction is different. There is a calmness tempered with understanding.

Healthy command phrases sound like this:
- "Tell me more"
- "I understand"
- "Let's talk about that"
- "That must have upset you"

JACK: Those sound so much more peaceful than the angry reactions. I was so good at.

ELI: Think about when President Kennedy was shot, or when the Challenger blew up, or 9-11? You probably can remember what you were doing, where you were, and what was said when you heard about at least one of these tragic events.

JACK: Sure can.

ELI: Most everyone can remember those traumatic events with great clarity. During 9-11, did you have strong emotions when you saw people jumping out of windows, the Twin Towers collapsing, and witnessing the fatigue on the firefighters' faces?

JACK: I can remember exactly what I was doing that morning. Why is that? And yeah, I had very strong emotions . . . anger, rage, shock, disgust were just a few.

ELI: Traumatic events create strong feelings and lead to emotional learning. These strong feelings glue the experience forever into memory. We do not forget those events. What happens to these command phrases you say to yourself in the heat of your anger?

JACK: They are also "glued" into your memory. I love that, "glued" into memory. That's rich.

ELI: Yes, they enter the unconscious mind as facts!

JACK: Is that what you called emotional learning?

ELI: Exactly. Now go back to that terrible night you described to me when your daughter tried to sneak out. Do you recall what you told me you were feeling? I've written it down if you'd like me to recall it for you.

JACK: Please do, I'd really like to forget that night . . . but I guess I can't.

ELI: Let's see . . . under the Mad feelings you were "angry, disapproving, enraged, furious, hostile, feeling rage, and under the other feelings you were "alarmed, fearful, frightened, horrified, hurt, burdened, disappointed, and in pain", sound right?

JACK: Yeah.

ELI: Often when emotionally drunk we are . . . RUI . . . "Reacting under the Influence"!

JACK: Oh, clever, not D U I —*Driving Under the Influence* but RUI—*Reacting Under the Influence*. Yeah, I spent a lot of time there.

ELI: When you were RUI, what were you saying to yourself when you were so full of emotions?

JACK: Like self-talk?

ELI: Yes.

JACK: "She can't do this to me!" "I'll teach her to have no respect for me!" "She thinks she runs this family but she doesn't!"

ELI: Let me write them into our model under the command phrase.

T.I.E. – Anger Management Model

Exhibit VII

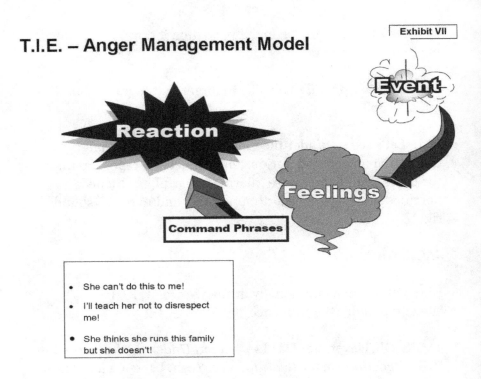

- She can't do this to me!
- I'll teach her not to disrespect me!
- She thinks she runs this family but she doesn't!

ELI: All of these statements fit into the Outward Focus category.

JACK: Yeah, and oh, one I just thought of . . . man, it's hard to say. This hurts even to recall. I was thinking my wife to proud of me on how well I handled this. Remember, she had lost respect for me.

ELI: You were handling this. . . protecting your daughter, and expecting your wife would be pleased with what a good father you were?

JACK: Yeah, sick wasn't it. Man, until this moment, I never thought of that.

ELI: Let me say it another way. Your best attempt to show love for your daughter and wife turned out disastrous.

JACK: Yeah, neither felt love.
ELI: How do you feel right now?

JACK: Sick . . . with lots of regret and shame. Hurt. Yeah, I feel hurt.

ELI: Hurt and pain. Sometimes we have to understand it differently before we can allow healing to happen.

JACK: I guess the results are what I am experiencing now. Kind of like a hangover after being emotionally drunk.

ELI: Well, said. So, using your hangover analogy, you now have a bad headache and are sick to your stomach with regret.

JACK: Yeah, I look forward to that healing you promised, although I don't see how they can forgive me or how I can forgive myself.

ELI: Actually you are working on forgiveness right now.

JACK: I am? How?

ELI: The forgiveness process has three parts. The first part is saying the words, admitting your error, and asking for forgiveness. The second part, and perhaps the hardest, is to be willing to listen to how your behavior affects the other person. That takes broad shoulders and not everyone is willing to endure that experience. I hope you have the opportunity to listen to them.

JACK: I would like that opportunity to make my amends, and I am now willing to listen to how my behavior made them feel. Yes, I'm ready. But you said I'm already working on forgiveness. How's that?

ELI: The third part of forgiveness, which you are working on, is to change behavior.

JACK: Making amends is not only saying the words but also being willing to listen, and then changing behavior.

ELI: You've got it.

JACK: Simple, but not easy. Do you think they will listen to what I was feeling?

ELI: They won't until you listen to them, will they?

JACK: Did you think up this concept of the command phrases?

ELI: No, they came from the book *How to Solve Problems and Prevent Trouble,* by Richard Wetherill.

JACK: Who came up with the "I over E" theory?

ELI: I don't know the author, but I learned the basics of it in a seminar. Over the years, I've added several parts to this model. When I read about the command phrases, they begged to be included in the model, so I borrowed them from Mr. Wetherill.

Okay, see you next week, Jack.

Chapter 6

Beliefs—Behavior Continuum

Sixth counseling session—November 7th

Beliefs – Behavior Continuum

Exhibit VIII

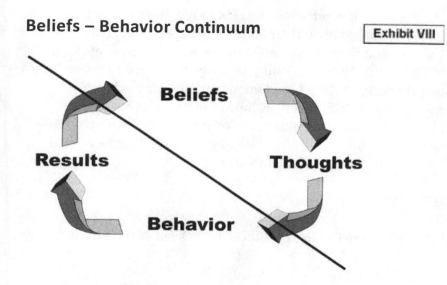

ELI: Good to see you, Jack. Let's start this session with the BBC Model. The bottom left half of this figure is obvious to most people. . . from behavior comes results. A student, who studies hard, attends classes, pays attention, will usually perform with greater results than one who goofs off. For the most part, this is a fact of life; the rewards belong to those who behave in a certain manner. Good behavior gets good results and bad behaviors are equally rewarding but with negative results.

JACK: Why is it called BBC?

ELI: Oh, that stands for *Beliefs—Behavior Continuum*. It's a collection of several other people's work such as Patrick Carnes and his Addictive Cycle, and Albert Ellis with his Rational Emotive Therapy. Like this one, so many theories are based upon other people's work. We each add a little more to the knowledge base.

JACK: So results follow behavior, what's the rest of this model?

ELI: Everyone has certain beliefs about life, their worldview. This view is based upon their education, experiences, parental messages, and their own thought processes. These beliefs tend to dictate their thinking. Faulty belief systems tend to cause faulty thinking. Beliefs based upon truth drastically improve thinking. Tying it all together, human behavior is based upon how a person thinks. A man sat upon a cactus and suffered the consequence of thorns. When asked why he did that he replied "It seemed like a good idea at the time!"

JACK: I know that cactus!

ELI: Yeah, we're trying to get those thorns out of your butt!

JACK: Thanks, I feel better already!

ELI: You're welcome. Now, to complete the cycle, the result of the behavior reinforces a person's belief system.

JACK: I get it. Until that belief system is challenged, the cycle continues, it doesn't matter if it is correct or not. We believe it is so because it fits our worldview.

ELI: Great. Now here's an example: take the elephant at the circus, when they are not performing they are kept outside the tent with a rope tied around one of their legs and anchored to the ground with a large stake. Just looking at that elephant, it would be logical to assume an animal that strong could break the rope, but they don't, how come?

JACK: Don't know.

ELI: When the elephant was a baby the same rope was tied to the same leg. The baby tugged and tugged on the rope but was not strong enough to break it. One day it learned that no matter how hard it pulled on the rope it was stuck. On that day, the baby elephant knew that when tied to a rope, escape was impossible.

JACK: What leg?

ELI: Now I really don't know, let's say the left one.

JACK: I'm pulling your chain; you're easy to do that with.

ELI: Yes, you are good at that. Some people are and you're one of them. You evidently have my combination!

JACK: Got you irritated?

ELI: Is it that obvious?

JACK: Are you "I over E" now?

ELI: I am now, and thanks for the reminder that I still need to work on the control of my own anger.

JACK: Control or management?

ELI: Management. You're learning very fast. Here . . . you hold the clipboard and be the therapist. I'll be the client.

Another example: When my nineteen-year-old son helped me give a talk to a singles group, I planned to use this model and showed it to him. After I explained the model, he said, "Oh, I know how that works. When I was ten, you told me I couldn't save money."

Sheepishly, I said, "I did?" And he said, "Yeah, you did." Although I did not remember the incident, I knew what he said was true. In my frustration with his ten-year-old lack of fiscal responsibility, I probably said that. What a message! Here was the man who he respected, and who loved him, making that statement. Dad said it, and then it must be true!

With that firmly embedded in his belief system, his thoughts were all about spending. And since thoughts dictate behavior, he never let a nickel stay long enough to burn a hole in his pocket. What was the result of spending everything he had? He was constantly broke! That result reinforced his belief system, that he could not save money.

When he told me that, I declared in my most emphatic voice: "Son, I was dead wrong, I truly believe you can save money!" Ten years later, he was laid off at his job. He did not call me for help because he used his SAVINGS!

JACK: Man, it sounds like you screwed up your kids as badly as I did mine! Then again, you had a chance and corrected that mistake.

ELI: Where do you think my wisdom comes from? It's from what I've done wrong and the lessons learned because of those mistakes. What I do now as a therapist is penance for all the harm I've done. It is my way of apologizing and making amends. Maybe, just maybe, I can help someone else avoid hurting someone. And when that happens, I can add a little more forgiveness toward myself.

JACK: I really appreciate what you just said. You're not perfect and have much regret, just like me.

ELI: More than you know, my friend.

JACK: Maybe I can forgive myself.

ELI: I know you can. If I can, I know you can!

JACK: I want to believe you.

ELI: Trust the process, keep working, and it'll happen.

JACK: Trust the process?

ELI: Yeah, trust the process!

Now think of the command phrases you used in the anger example. As I recall, it was: "She can't do this to me! I'll teach her to disrespect me! She thinks she runs this family but she doesn't!"

JACK: And don't forget "My wife will respect me for the way I'm handling this."

ELI: How could I forget?

JACK: Remember, we have established that you are not perfect!

ELI: Yes, I'm not perfect. Definitely not. Not Gandhi, Lincoln, or MLK.

JACK: Human.

ELI: Yeah. I've committed more than my share of mistakes.

JACK: You don't have a retro-spectra-scope?

ELI: If I had one, knowing me back then, I would not have used it!

See, I knew better. I had the answers. If you don't believe me, just ask me and I'll set you straight.

But let's get back . . . those command phrases were embedded into your belief system in the moments of strong emotions. Your subconscious mind now has those command phrases as your truth.

JACK: So that is why what I think is real . . . because it is embedded in my emotional memory?

ELI: Exactly.

Like when we are angry with our boss and call him a "jerk" under our breath. In our subconscious mind, over time and with repetition, that definition becomes a belief about him. Then whenever we think about the boss, our subconscious mind searches for his image and comes up with the belief that says, "Jerk!" If that belief were strongly held, how would it affect the way we interact with him?

JACK: I would expect him to be a jerk and would look for evidence that proves my belief.

ELI: You got it! When we are emotionally drunk, what we say to ourselves and to others often has lasting and sometimes devastating effects.

JACK: Wow! All the horrible messages I've given to those I love. My gut hurts!

ELI: Words are powerful, especially when they affect those who are close to us.

JACK: I need to go home and lick my wounds.

ELI: Think about that for a moment. If you are operating out of excessive guilt . . . are you emotionally sober or emotionally drunk?

JACK: I see what you are saying . . . not forgiving myself keeps me emotionally drunk.

ELI: That is correct. . . shall we make another appointment?

JACK: Absolutely!

Chapter 7

Smorgasbord

Seventh counseling session—November 12th

JACK: Okay, I'm back for another lesson. What's on the menu today?

ELI: Funny you should ask. Today I have a banquet for you. It's a smorgasbord of some other wonderful anger management tools you can use while you count to ten.

JACK: I love smorgasbord; did you know I'm one-half Swedish?

ELI: Really, so am I.

Okay, now let's start with the appetizer. How do you breathe when you are angry? How do you breathe when you are anxious?

JACK: Breathe? . . . When I'm angry or anxious . . . hmmm . . . it's with short and quick breaths . . . almost a pant. Sometimes, if I'm mad enough I don't breathe at all!

ELI: That's right, when someone is angry they breathe shallow and rapidly. However, when we breathe deeply and slowly, a corresponding calming effect occurs. This calmness helps us to manage those strong emotions.

You can tell how deeply you are breathing by watching your stomach. If it rises when you inhale, you will experience an enjoyable relaxing sensation.

JACK: How do you do that?

ELI: Put your hands on your stomach . . . now breathe deeply. . . get your stomach to push your hands up.

JACK: My stomach has been pushing up all by itself for years!

ELI: Well, many people suck in their stomachs when breathing and it is hard to change that habit and push out instead.

Okay, now take three or four deep breaths as you get your stomach to push up when you breathe . . . deeply and slowly.

JACK: Yeah, doing deep breathing really works, I do feel rather relaxed.

> *Use deep breathing to manage strong emotions,*
> *such as anger and anxiety.*

ELI: For many years, I taught a court-ordered anger management course for the Baton Rouge City Court. Part of the course curriculum was teaching deep breathing. After demonstrating this principle in one session, one participant came back the second day with this story:

He said, "I came home very late and discovered I was locked out of my house! I felt rage boiling up inside of me. I was going to bust down that door! I thought, 'They can't do that to me!' Then I remembered to use deep breathing.

I want you to picture this". . . he went on to say, "It is 2:30 in the morning, I'm in my backyard locked out of my house, doing deep breathing and I'm thinking about you, Eli!"

By doing the deep breathing, he was able to calm down enough to do something appropriate, like maybe knock on the door.

JACK: Deep breathing can do that?

And he was thinking about you. He doesn't sound like someone I would want to be thinking about me.

ELI: True. I hadn't thought about that until you mentioned it.

So now, let's continue the smorgasbord with the salad. If a person is sitting down in a chair and someone says something disrespectful, what might you expect their reaction to be?

JACK: Instant anger, especially if they were emotionally drunk!

ELI: Correct. Would they remain sitting or would they get on their feet?

JACK: They would jump up to confront this insult, right?

ELI: Right. They would jump up . . . getting to our feet is a normal reaction when our anger is triggered.

JACK: That is a natural protection, getting ready for fighting or running away.

ELI: Correct. We stand up when we are angry, probably because the anger is providing a warning. We are not that many generations removed from swinging out of the trees expecting to be attacked by "lions, and tigers, and bears"!

JACK: Oh, my! Are we still in Kansas, Toto?

ELI: How we physically react can help us to manage our emotions.

When we want to manage our anger, we can do the opposite of what the anger tells us. Instead of standing up, we can remain seated . . . or if we're already standing, we can just sit down.

JACK: Like when we see the weigh-in of a professional boxing match and the two fighters go nose to nose staring at each other, trying intimidation tactics or before two guys get into a schoolyard fight, there is a lot of posturing, like stepping forward into the other guy's space.

Exactly, if you find yourself in that situation and want to de-escalate the probability of going to "fist-city", take a step backward. This does not decrease your ability to defend yourself, but it does send a message that you are willing to diffuse the situation.

JACK: The message is "I'm willing if you're willing."

ELI: And hopefully, the other person will want a way out of the conflict. So by stepping back you provide the space, the reason, to slow the action.

JACK: Hopefully, indeed.

ELI: Here's a little lagniappe. (/'laenjaep/_LAN-yap_)

JACK: A lawn-a-who?

ELI: It's what Cajun people say. . . It means providing something extra. The kids want their "lagniappe" when they are in the grocery store, usually in the form of candy.

JACK: Okay, so what's the lagniappe today?

ELI: Let's use your ex-wife for the example.

JACK: Do we have to? Just kidding.

ELI: Okay, when she would get angry, what would you do?

JACK: Of course. . . I'd get angry . . . I didn't know I had a choice.

ELI: Well, here is something you can say to yourself whenever the opportunity occurs. So when she's angry, now you will know you have a choice. . . you can get angry with her, or you can use this wonderful little statement. . . a phrase from the book, *Crucial Conversations*. . . "You can get furious. . . or. . . you can get curious." The co-author, Kerry Patterson, calls it a "Decision Question".

Remember that you can choose to be angry . . . or you can choose not to be angry.

JACK: I got that one. It's up to me.

You told me in our very first session that life is simple . . . not easy, but simple.

ELI: We're not talking rocket science here.

JACK: So, if I choose to be curious, then I have to wonder why she is angry. Instead of reacting to her anger, I can be curious about her feelings.

ELI: Right.

JACK: You know, although I didn't know about this technique, I actually did that the other day.

ELI: You did? Tell me about it.

JACK: Well, she called me when she was angry about something, and instead of reacting to her anger as I normally did, I listened. Because I was listening, I did not hear the anger. This time I heard something that was beneath her anger.

ELI: What did you hear?

JACK: I heard fear. All these years I thought she was an angry person. She wasn't angry. She was fearful. When I heard the fear, I reacted differently and said, "This is scary for you." Know what she said?

ELI: What?

JACK: She said "Yes, I am afraid,". . . and then we talked about what was so frightening for her.

ELI: Instead of getting furious, you got curious.

JACK: Yeah.

ELI: That fits into another little gem.

JACK: Another? You collect these gems of wisdom.

ELI: Right, I can't be much help to others if I don't have some tools that work.

JACK: You're giving me my money's worth.

ELI: Glad you think so.

Take the example you just gave. Your normal pattern of conversation would be to react angrily, correct?

JACK: Yeah, I'd have jumped all over her.

ELI: If you had "jumped all over her", you would have bitten the bait she put out for you.

JACK: The bait?

ELI: Yes, the invitation to join them in chaos. People often get into patterns, recognizable patterns of how they deal with one another. She says this and you do that, or you do this and she says that. A pattern. It's as if you two are in a dance and you both know the steps so well, you're doing them unconsciously or by rote. If I were watching you dance, it would be a graceful dance because you have danced together for so long. Unless you told me, just watching you glide across the dance floor, I wouldn't know if it was a painful dance for one or both of you.

JACK: Like a dance of anger.

ELI: Correct. In fact, this little analogy came from a book entitled *The Dance of Anger* by Dr. Harriet Lerner.

JACK: My steps sure were painful, and I guess her steps were as well.

ELI: And yet you both kept dancing.

JACK: For twenty years . . . that same painful dance.

ELI: Well, many people make that choice. When people come in for marriage counseling it's because the steps have become too painful. They seldom seek counseling when things are wonderful. They come in expecting some relief, but often flee the process when they discover they have to take action, and do something to make the pain go away.

Change is hard. The process of learning to act in responsible ways can be overwhelming. There is a strong tendency to go back to their old dance steps rather than to make changes. Only when you start to choose do you have a choice.

JACK: I'd never have come here if she hadn't kicked me out.

ELI: Exactly. So, the person with the painful dance steps has three choices. One is to continue the old painful but familiar dance steps . . . remember change can be frightening. The second choice is to develop new dance steps. If that happens, one person has the old steps and the other is dancing new steps, so the dance has now become awkward.

It is easy to see when treating substance abuse clients. If one person in a relationship enters treatment, attends a 12-Step program, and makes significant changes, and the other one does not, it puts tremendous pressure on the relationship. This is why most marriages break up in active recovery, not during the active addiction phase!

The third choice of this Dance of Anger is to stop dancing.

JACK: That's what she did, she quit dancing with me.

ELI: Right. But let's look at her other options. She could have continued dancing the old steps as she'd been doing for so many years, or she could have developed new steps that were no longer painful, and hoped you would change yours.

JACK: So, if I had changed my dance steps there was a chance she might have had a corresponding positive change.

ELI: There are no guarantees, but that's a distinct possibility.

Sometimes I have people phone me for marriage counseling and their partner refuses to participate.

JACK: What do you do then?

ELI: I tell them that one person can have a tremendous affect on changing the relationship. Take you and your ex-wife for example. What percentage of the problem between the two of you was hers and what part was yours?

JACK: When I first came in here, I thought it was entirely mine, but you have opened my eyes. I'd say now it was closer to fifty-fifty.

ELI: Okay, let's say that your part of the problem was fifty percent. If you worked on solving your part of the problem, what happens to the size of the problem? Is it larger or smaller?

JACK: Smaller, of course.

ELI: Right. She may not have done a bit of work on her part, but what is separating the two of you now is a much smaller problem, now a good deal easier to deal with.

JACK: I just change my dance steps.

ELI: It's that simple.

Mad	Glad	Sad	Fear	Hurt
Agitated	Admiration	Abandoned	Alarm	Aloof
Angry	Affection	Agonized	Anxious	Ashamed
Annoyed	Ardor	Bored	Apprehensive	Belittled
Antagonized	Confident	Crushed	Bashful	Burdened
Arrogant	Cordiality	Deflated	Bewildered	Cheated
Bitter	Curiosity	Depressed	Cautious	Denied
Contemptuous	Delight	Disconnected	Confused	Deserted
Defiant	Desire	Disparaged	Distracted	Disappointed
Disapproving	Devotion	Distant	Dread	Dismay
Disdainful	Ecstasy	Distraught	Embarrassed	Embarrassed
Disgust	Elation	Distressed	Envious	Exhausted
Enraged	Enthusiasm	Downcast	Evasive	Guilty
Flustered	Excitement	Forlorn	Fearful	Humiliated
Frustrated	Fervor	Gloomy	Flustered	Insulted
Furious	Flushed	Grieving	Frightened	Lonely
Hostile	Generosity	Helpless	Horrified	Mean
indignant	Happy	Hopeless	Hysterical	Pained
Irritated	Hopeful	Ignored	Inadequate	Regret
Livid	Inspired	Isolated	Insecure	Shame
Rage	Love-Struck	Jealous	Meanced	Suffering
Resentful	Passion	Melancholy	Overwhelmed	
	Pride	Miserable	Panic	
	Sympathy	Mournful	Pathos	
	Thrilled	Remorseful	Shocked	
		Unwanted		

ELI: Now for the meat and potatoes. Look at all those feeling words on the feeling chart.

When a person experiences any of these emotions, there is energy associated with each one. Some feelings have more energy than others do. One of the simplest but most effective methods of maintaining emotional sobriety is to express what you are feeling. Just start saying aloud what you are feeling. For example, "I'm feeling angry, resentful, hurt, disgusted!"

Instead of feeling words, often a person says, "I feel like . . ." That is a dead giveaway that they are expressing a thought and not an actual feeling. So be sure you are using the actual feeling words found on the feeling chart.

JACK: Wait a minute, you mean just by saying these words aloud, I can manage my emotions? I'm sorry, Eli, but that is hard to believe.

ELI: It may be hard to believe, but it is true.

I had a couple in my office. The man was as mad as anyone who has ever been there. He couldn't sit down, he was hollering at his wife, cursing, shaking his fist at her. I put the feeling chart in his face and said, "What are you feeling?" He just pushed my hand away and continued to berate his cowering wife. I again stuck the chart in his face and raised my voice. "What are you feeling?" He again pushed my arm away and this time cursed at me. Again I put that chart in his face, and cussed back at him . . . I called that technique "therapeutic-cursing" . . . and demanded that he tell me what he was feeling!

JACK: I can see you cursing at him!

ELI: He grabbed the chart and hollered, "I'm angry! Hurt! Enraged!

Humiliated!" What was amazing to see, was that with each word he said, his overinflated physical bearing decreased, just like a balloon when the air is slowly released. In a few moments, he sat down, and I thanked him for letting us know what he was feeling.

Just saying the words is a wonderful release of energy, allowing the calmness to return, and sobriety to find its way back.

JACK: So by saying the words aloud, I can maintain my emotional sobriety?

ELI: Yes, and again that simple.

JACK: I need to have one of those feeling charts with me at all times.

ELI: The chart helps, but all you really need is five words: Mad, Glad, Sad, Hurt, and Fear.

JACK: So, it really is all so very simple.

ELI: Not rocket science. Simple . . . but not easy.

JACK: Simple, just don't become negative.

ELI: Exactly. Just remember that negativity and happiness cannot exist in the same person at the same time.

JACK: Wow! Now that is profound. I can choose to be negative but if I do, by that action I have chosen not to be happy.

ELI: You've got it.

JACK: It's my choice.

ELI: Your choice.

JACK: What's next for dinner, when do we get to have dessert?

ELI: Not now! We have to eat our vegetables.

I once worked for a counseling agency. The very first day I was there, the office manager told me about her pet peeve. She said, "I hate to come into the bathroom and see the commode seat lifted. Will you remember to lower it?" In this office we had only one bathroom, so I understood her concern. I like it when people tell me what they need, so I granted her request. For three years, I faithfully lowered the commode seat. I was proud of myself!

JACK: Proud. . . for putting down the toilet seat?

ELI: Yep, proud of myself. One day when I finished, my usual practice after washing my hands was to lower the commode seat, but that day I was mad at her.

I thought, "I'm never going to lower the toilet seat again. In fact, I'll go in after others and raise the commode seat!" Fortunately, a little sentence flashed through my mind that said, "If you don't speak it out, you'll tend to act it out."

So, I lowered the seat, went into her office, and said, "I have a problem." By doing that, I didn't have to act it out!

I told this story to a teenage girl and she looked at me, smiled, and said, "I've been lifting a lot of commode seats!"

Lifting commode seats is passive aggressive behavior and is an indirect expression of strong emotions.

JACK: Well, I've certainly lifted my share of commode seats!

ELI: Until we have that wonderful little sentence, "If you don't speak it out, you'll tend to act it out", it is easy to do.

JACK: So vegetables are like commode seats?

ELI: I'm not going there! Now we get to the dessert.

JACK: I thought you'd never get here.

ELI: A good question that comes out of the 12- Step movement is, "How important is it?" It is a powerful question to ask. My son learned to assess his anger by putting a point value to the circumstances. He ranks each situation from one to ten with ten being the most severe, and one very insignificant. What was amazing to him was that he was expressing anger at situations he had only rated as twos and threes!

JACK: You know, as I think about it, I'll bet most of my anger is also about the small numbers! How ridiculous!

ELI: If everything seems important, then nothing is important. Until we practice discernment, our mental stress is increased as we place the required energy onto all these competing demands.

JACK: I have to admit it but I wasted a lot of energy on unimportant things and my stress increases unnecessarily.

ELI: One of my clients created a question she would ask herself when she faced multiple demands: "Is anyone going to die if I do not react to this?" If no one was in danger of getting blood on the ground, she relaxed and asked of each competing demand, "How important is it? Will someone die?"

JACK: So is that it? Are we finished with the smorgasbord?

ELI: Not quite. In some cultures, it is considered impolite unless there is a belch in appreciation of the meal. Therefore, we need...

JACK: A Burp?

ELI: As we did in the third grade when burps and farts were fascinating.

So, here's our burp: If you ever listen to radio or cable TV talk show hosts, most have a certain attitude. They can be a flaming liberal, or politically to the right of Genghis Khan. It doesn't matter. Most demonstrate this trait.

JACK: As in, "I' m right, and anyone who disagrees with me is wrong?"

ELI: Yes. These electronic personalities express their opinions as facts. If they say something with enough emphasis, with enough conviction, and then repeat it often enough, what they say becomes fact to them, and often in the minds of their listeners.

JACK: You're not saying they are opinionated are you?

ELI: Indeed, I am. I see our country becoming increasingly more polarized. This polarization, this black and white point of view, or all or nothing thinking, creates a great potential for conflict. It occurs when we hold absolute positions and do not allow or respect the beliefs of others. In a political spectrum, listen to what the speaker is really screaming: "I'm right and you're wrong".

JACK: You get pretty worked up about this, don't you?

ELI: Perhaps, but when opinions are expressed as facts then they must be defended. Anger is often the emotion used to convey this defense. That puts people on opposite sides of an argument and creates hostility. Politics and religion are two topics fraught with opinions we think we must defend as absolutes. If a person is emotionally drunk and is into absolutism, there is little room for understanding or healthy debate and communication ceases . . . a recipe for disaster.

Do you know what the world's largest addictions are?

JACK: Alcohol and gambling?

ELI: No, not even close . . . The two largest addictions affecting more people are . . . . Looking good, and being right!

JACK: Ha! All of us have one or both of those.

ELI: My counselor used to say that.

JACK: You've been to counseling?

ELI: Sure, doing just what you are doing, working on improving myself. I've also been to many 12- Step programs. Let me tell you . . . Eli is a work in progress!

JACK: So, you are not perfect, and you still need help.

ELI: We established that previously!

JACK: Am I committing myself to a lifetime of work on Jack?

ELI: Only if you choose to commit. Life is about choices.

Looking good, and being right. You see this problem with opinionated talk show hosts. They are so certain that what they say is correct; they are totally convinced they are right! They want to look good by being right, they want that sense of omnipotence. When awarded with a worshipful audience, they begin to see their own faces in the constellations. Put this compulsive need to be right together with an over-inflated ego and guess what happens if anyone has a contrary opinion?

JACK: Arguments happen. Those talk show hosts do not seem to be happy people. To maintain that angry edge they also have to be negative, and as you say, "Negativity and happiness cannot exist in the same person at the same time!"

ELI: You learn well. How about in a close relationship? Does having to be right cause problems?

JACK: It did in mine.

ELI: Think of the times you and your wife argued.

JACK: The thousands of times?

ELI: If you are very honest, and are looking down on yourself from above during one of your arguments, how much of the quarrel is about the topic of disagreement, and how much of it is just you arguing about your need to be right?

JACK: Most of it is about my being right . . . now that I think about it. I think she also argued to be right.

ELI: When my wife and I first got married, she presented a slogan sentence that really helped us not fall into the "being right" trap.

JACK: Hey, that trap is where I live!

ELI: Is that where you want to be? Would you like to move?

Here is the little sentence that offers a completely different awareness . . .

JACK: Do I need a drum roll for this one too?

ELI: Yes, maestro . . . Hit it!

JACK: Ka-boom, ka-boom, ka-boom!

ELI: Here it is: "Would you rather be right . . . or would you rather be happy?"

JACK: Oh, I'm happy when I'm right! Man, there are many times we fought over such stupid, silly things, and I thought they were so important but it was really my need to be right. Somehow, if I could prove my "rightness" to her obvious "wrongness" then with my shallow self-esteem, I could feel better. By putting her down somehow, I would feel better.

ELI: So, being right . . . did it work for you?

JACK: Not at all, because even when I won the fight, even when I could prove my magnificence compared to her . . . in the end, I lost.

ELI: Even when you won, you lost what an insight that is!

JACK: So many wasted moments, wasted opportunities, and my God, a lot of wasted love. I wonder what had happened if instead of arguing with her, I just held her hand and discussed our differences?

ELI: How beautiful, maybe you could use that technique in your future?

JACK: Thank you for all your help.

ELI: You are welcome.

Chapter 8

Jack's Notes

September 30th

- When you use anger correctly, you get positive results.

- Anger has two benefits: it provides a warning and the necessary energy for change.

- All feelings are based upon the thoughts we have.

- Anger is a natural feeling.

- Anger can enslave us, or it can provide freedom, all depending upon how it is used.

- No one can make you angry! No one can make you mad! You get to choose.

- There is freedom knowing that anger is a choice.

October 7th

- If someone else is angry, you have a choice to be angry or not—this is freedom!

- Your feelings do not lie to you, however they may be based upon:

    o False thought
    o True thought
    o Incomplete information

- If a person changes their thinking, it can have a great effect on their reactions.

- When confronted with strong emotions, especially anger, repeating to yourself "I over E" (Intellect over Emotions) is an excellent way to maintaining your cool.

- We are as sick as our secrets.

October 15th

- "My Life Will Change . . . When I Change"™

- Locus of Control is where people place their personal power:

    o External—blaming others—victim mentality
    o Internal—being responsible—responsible for changing self

- In the end, no one can make anyone happy. A person's happiness is their responsibility not yours.

- Listing someone else's faults is taking someone else's inventory, and usually starts conflict.

- Expectations are resentments under construction.

- Rather than pointing fingers, focus on our thumbs:
    - Finger Work = creates resentments
    - Thumb work = makes changes in ourselves

October 21st

- There are five basic words in the feeling language: Mad, Sad, Glad, Hurt, Fear

- Emotionally numb people are:
    - Heading in the wrong direction
    - Not real / not alive
    - Unhappy

- All decisions involve emotions, ignoring emotions decreases the quality of the result.

- When we acknowledge our feelings, we can use them like an internal radar set to guide us.

- When we are not connected with our emotions, we are not connected to ourselves.

- A command phrase is an internal message of what we tell ourselves, and is embedded into our belief system when associated with strong emotions. Unless these phrases are challenged, they become our truth, what we believe.

- Self-forgiveness is a choice.

- Strong feelings associated with an event can keep memories alive forever.

- RUI—Reacting Under the Influence—This happens when we are emotionally drunk and automatically react to something or someone.

November 7th

- From our behavior, we obtain certain results, and these results reinforce our beliefs. What we think is based upon on how we see life, our beliefs.

- Not forgiving yourself is a form of being emotionally drunk.

November 12th

- Deep breathing creates a calming effect to help manage strong emotions such as anger or anxiety.

- To de-escalate a potential conflict, one method is to take a step backwards.

- A great tool from the book, Crucial Conversations is: "You can get furious or curious". You can get mad, or choose to wonder why this person is behaving the way they are.

- It is only when you start to choose . . . do you have a choice.

- In the book: Dance of Anger there are three recognizable patterns to a conflict:

    o Continue old dance steps
    o Develop new dance steps
    o Stop dancing.

- If you don't speak it out, you'll then act it out. Example: lifting the commode seat to express anger.

- A good question to gain perspective in life is: How important is it?

- Emotionally drunk people stuck in absolutism decreases communication and understanding and creates polarization. . . a recipe for disaster

- What is the largest addiction in the world? Looking good and being right!

- Life is all about choices.

- "Would you rather be right . . . . or would you rather be happy?"

Chapter 9

Epilogue

The therapy sessions end as Jack and Eli go their separate ways. Or do they? Actually, it is now time to confess, to reveal the actual

Identities of these two men who by means of their dialogue guided us through this anger management method.

As I mentioned in the beginning, both these men are real people, and these are their original words. Although the original descriptions of Jack and Eli are true, they are somewhat deceptive. Whether I am to be condemned or understood for why I constructed this little deception, you be the judge.

In case you have not yet guessed it . . . both men are me. I gave them false identities and names. They are separated by over twenty years of experience and wisdom. Jack is me in my early forties when I was wrestling with the addictions of both of my children, a failed marriage, and the loss of my business.

Eli is me, in my mid-sixties with much more experience, but to my great surprise still remorseful about my reaction back when my daughter tried to sneak out. I know there were many other times where my anger hurt family members, but this one sticks out as the most memorable and most painful.

Writing about that night, I underwent a great deal of personal healing. Through this dialectic exercise, I was able to work through that experience. I did not expect healing's release, but I am grateful to have received the peace of self-forgiveness I so long sought.

Chapter 10

Anger Management Model Workbook

A key tool in managing emotions is found in the T.I.E Model for Anger Management. You experienced it with Jack and Eli now it is presented as a pure theory uncluttered with dialogue. This anger management model includes nine exhibits providing a systematic process for learning this simple but powerful model. Although at first it may look intimidating, but as Jack experienced, it is really quite simple and it absolutely works. It will change your life!

How to use this workbook model:

Go through each exhibit. First look at the model and notice how it has changed from the previous exhibit. Then read how it works and complete the small exercise that is associated with each exhibit.

How it Works:

Because of important events, all humans have certain feelings. These next exercises will provide a framework to assist you in managing strong emotions; not to deny but to manage them.

Exercise:

Think of a time when you became angry, lost it, locked your jaws, and got very uptight! It does not have to be a recent event, just memorable. Write down a thumbnail sketch of the event. Briefly, what happened?

How it Works:

The major words in the feeling language are Mad, Glad, Sad, Fear, and Hurt. The feeling list on page 96 has five columns with one of these words at the top of each column. This chart represents the rainbow of emotions available to be experienced in the human condition.

Exercise:

Have the event that made you angry have firmly in your mind, and then look at the mood chart to find which feelings you were experiencing (use only words on this list).

Write down all the feelings you were experiencing. First list the "Mad" feelings, then in a separate column write all the other feelings you experienced under the Sad, Fear, and Hurt columns on the feeling chart. Spend some time identifying what emotions you experienced.

Mad	Other Feeling

T.I.E. – Anger Management Model

How it Works:

When a person experiences an event, various feelings are generated. With strong feelings, an equally strong reaction often occurs when something is said, or other action is taken, that would not have happened with a cooler mind. The reaction could be something said that is not really meant, a physical attack, or maybe the silent treatment.

Exercise:

What was your reaction to the identified event in the previous example? If you were observing YOU, what would you have witnessed? Did you yell, try to hurt someone else, run, get silent, plan revenge, or act out in some other equally dramatic way?

If you were observing you, what would you have seen?

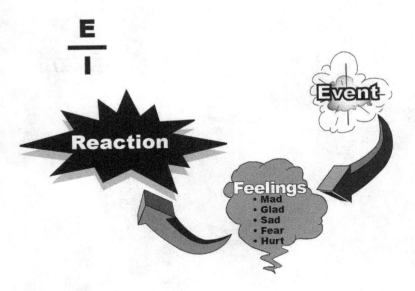

How it Works:

Unmanaged emotions create a reaction where there is a distinct possibility of hurting others emotionally, physically, and/or spiritually. This creates the condition where emotions are controlling intelligence, or as stated in the model above, "E over I".

When a person's emotions are controlling them, it is very similar to a person drunk with alcohol. For the purposes of this lesson, people who are "E over I" are labeled "emotionally drunk".

Exercise:

Think of all the damage you have done to people you care about, and to yourself when you have been emotionally drunk.

Has being emotionally drunk ever worked toward building successful relationships? Maybe, but is there a better way?

T.I.E. – Anger Management Model

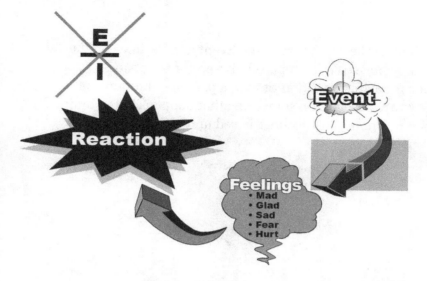

How it Works:

How often have you ever heard someone say, "He makes me so angry!" or "She irritates the fire out of me!" Would you like some freedom? The truth is no one (drum roll please) no one can make you angry; no one can irritate you!

By now you may want your money back on this book, but please do not reject this wonderful but simple truth. No one is in control of your emotions but you. Now that is freedom!

Exercise:

Do you want to continue reacting, or should a big red "X" be drawn through the E over I? Do you want to live emotionally drunk or emotionally sober? Your choice.

Now look at the line between the Event and Feelings on the diagram above. What happens between the event and a person's feelings? Saying it a different way, a person's emotions, or feelings are based upon something that happens in the brain. What are emotions or feelings based upon?

Take a guess.

T.I.E. – Anger Management Model

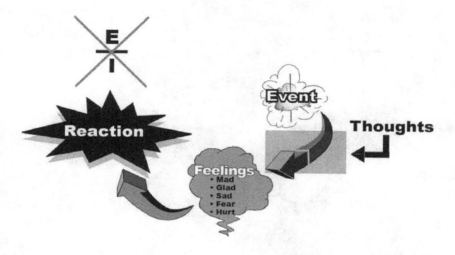

How it Works:

You guessed it — T H O U G H T S ! A person's thoughts cause emotions. When experiencing the identified event, certain thoughts are generated about that event, and those thoughts generated certain feelings. If we are not careful; BO OM, we have a reaction!

Exercise:

Holiday—No exercise required.

T.I.E. – Anger Management Model

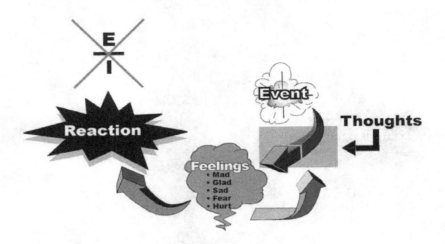

How it Works:

Look at the angry feelings listed under the Mad section. These are what we call "surface feelings". They are like the tip of the iceberg, what you see and observe. Under the angry feelings, there are other emotions as found in the Sad, Hurt, and/or fear columns. These other feelings are what is driving the strong reaction called anger.

Exercise:

Look at the feelings you listed in Exhibit X. Remember, you put the angry ones in one column and all the rest in another. Look at all the feelings not listed in the angry column. Identify the main feeling(s) driving your reaction. What feeling(s) has the most energy or best describes your emotional state? Select one or two.

Now think . . . what were the thoughts that were causing you to feel that emotion? Write your thoughts down.

Exhibit XVI

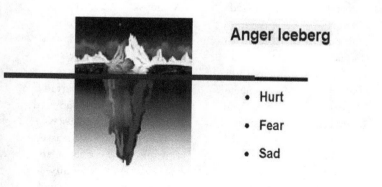

Anger Iceberg

- Hurt
- Fear
- Sad

There is a very good reason to separate the angry feelings as listed under the Mad column from the other columns of feelings. Anger is a surface feeling. Just like the iceberg, what you see is only the tip of the iceberg showing out of the water with most of it hidden beneath the water. In order to identify the strongest emotions driving our anger, we must dive beneath the waves and explore the Hurt, Fear, and Sad feelings.

Mad	Glad	Sad	Fear	Hurt
Agitated	Admiration	Abandoned	Alarm	Aloof
Angry	Affection	Agonized	Anxious	Ashamed
Annoyed	Ardor	Bored	Apprehensive	Belittled
Antagonized	Confident	Crushed	Bashful	Burdened
Arrogant	Cordiality	Deflated	Bewildered	Cheated
Bitter	Curiosity	Depressed	Cautious	Denied
Contemptuous	Delight	Disconnected	Confused	Deserted
Defiant	Desire	Disparaged	Distracted	Disappointed
Disapproving	Devotion	Distant	Dread	Dismay
Disdainful	Ecstasy	Distraught	Embarrassed	Embarrassed
Disgust	Elation	Distressed	Envious	Exhausted
Enraged	Enthusiasm	Downcast	Evasive	Guilty
Flustered	Excitement	Forlorn	Fearful	Humiliated
Frustrated	Fervor	Gloomy	Flustered	Insulted
Furious	Flushed	Grieving	Frightened	Lonely
Hostile	Generosity	Helpless	Horrified	Me
indignant	Happy	Hopeless	Hysterical	Pained
Irritated	Hopeful	Ignored	Inadequate	Regret
Rage	Love-Struck	Jealous	Menaced	Suffering
Resentful	Passion	Melancholy	Overwhelmed	
	Prid	Miserable	Panic	
	Sympathy	Mournful	Pathos	
	Thrilled	Remorseful	Shocked	
		Unwanted		

T.I.E. – Anger Management Model

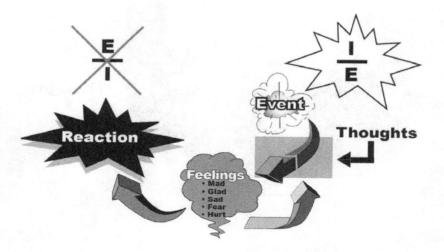

How it Works:

Once a person understands the thoughts that are driving their feelings, their intellect is now in control, and they are managing their emotions.

When managing emotions, that person is "I over E"; they are emotionally sober.

Exercise:

Take a deep breath. What often causes stress in people's life is that they do not know they have options. When you learn this technique, you now have choices. You can choose to be emotionally drunk or emotionally sober.

T.I.E. – Anger Management Model

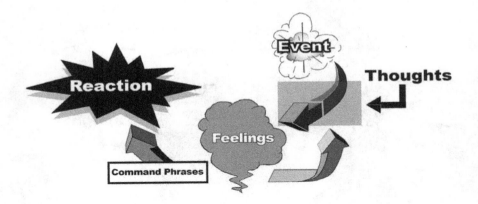

How it Works:

Go back to your anger incident previously identified.

In that anger incident you described, you were loaded with strong emotions that you probably did not manage well. When we react in the "emotionally drunk" state, allowing these emotions to be in control, we get the tag of "RUI" (reacting under intoxication). Often when we are in RUI", there is some illogical thinking associated.

Exercise:

What were you saying to yourself when you were so full of emotions?

List some of those thoughts.

T.I.E. – Anger Management Model

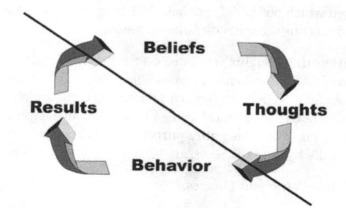

Beliefs

Results

Thoughts

Behavior

Command Phrases

Because of emotional learning, what we state to ourselves or to others when we are emotionally drunk becomes learned truths, indelibly printed in our minds, a very powerful form of learning.

This learning becomes our reality; out beliefs are based upon our thoughts and behaviors, as shown in the BBC

Model to the right.

Faulty belief results in harmful behaviors that we are often not able to see.

Review your Command Phrases, what would your behavior be if any one of these were your beliefs? Knowing where certain beliefs come from allows us to challenge them, thus freeing us from their control. This allows us to have a happier and more satisfying life.

When we are highly charged with emotions, our learning becomes sharper. Remember where you were and what you felt during 9-11. What we state to ourselves or express to others when we are full of emotions, as in being "emotionally drunk", becomes permanently printed in our mind. This is a very powerful form of learning. This learning becomes the reality upon which our beliefs are based. Thoughts come from beliefs and it is our thoughts dictating behavior.

Review the thoughts you listed on the previous page when you were RU I. What behavior would likely come from those thoughts? Knowing where certain beliefs come from enables us to challenge them, thus freeing ourselves to live happier and ore satisfying lives. The entire purpose of this book is improving your life by the skill necessary to manage powerful emotions.

Sample Command Phrases:

- I can't do anything right"

- "Don't depend upon anyone."

- "I try and I always fail"

- "I have more problems that I can solve."

- "I'm so stressed out ."

- "I'm going crazy."

- "She's such a bitch."

- "He is driving me nuts."

- "They are out to get me."

- "I can't take it!"

- "I can't control my emotions."

- "I'm at the end of my rope."

- "I hate my job."

- "The people here are all losers."

- "No one can push me around."

- "Nobody respects me."

- "No one listens to me."

- "They always get their way."

- "My boss is such a jerk."

About the Author

David W. Earle has twenty-five years of executive management experience in the construction field. He now earns his living as a Business Coach, working with individuals and organizations to improve human relationship skills, communication abilities, and leadership principals. Here, he assists clients in creating the changes they want to make in their businesses and in their personal lives.

He earned a Master's of Science in Counseling from Texas A&M. He is a mental health counselor licensed by the State of Louisiana, actively practicing since 1992. His practice covers such issues as substance abuse, compulsive gambling, relationships, families, adolescence, anxiety, and depression. For ten years, he worked for the Baton Rouge City Court teaching an anger management to a court-ordered population.

For 11 years, he was on the faculty of the University of Phoenix, teaching graduate courses in Conflict Management Systems and undergraduate courses on communications, employee motivation, diversity, sociology, and workplace substance abuse.

When bank robberies, suicides, explosions, sudden death, or disasters occur, David performs Critical Incident Stress Debriefing (C I S D) to assist traumatized employees. In addition, David works with the local Red Cross mental health disaster team.

David has been on the panel as a mediator and/or arbitrator for various organizations such as U.S. Federal Court-Middle District, Louisiana Rehabilitation Service, Equal Employment Opportunity Commission (EEOC), Financial Industry Regulator Authority (FINRA), and National Association of Security Dealers (NASD), Natural Futures Association (NFA), Federal Deposit Insurance Corporation (FDIC), and the Louisiana Supreme Court.

He enjoys tennis and he lives in Baton Rouge with his wife, Penny, and their dog, Fletcher, and cat, Hobbes.

Contact: David W. Earle, LPC - Lessonsbeforeliving@gmail.com

CPSIA information can be obtained
at www.ICGtesting.com
Printed in the USA
LVHW111310121020
668578LV00001B/176